Greater Than a Tourist
from Readers

I think the series is wonderful and beneficial for tourists to get information before visiting the city.

-Seckin Zumbul, Izmir Turkey

I am a world traveler who has read many trip guides but this one really made a difference for me. I would call it a heartfelt creation of a local guide expert instead of just a guide.

-Susy, Isla Holbox, Mexico

New to the area like me, this is a must have!

-Joe, Bloomington, USA

This is a good series that gets down to it when looking for things to do at your destination without having to read a novel for just a few ideas.

-Rachel, Monterey, USA

Good information to have to plan my trip to this destination.

-Pennie Farrell, Mexico

Velimir Ilicic

Aptly titled, you won't just be a tourist after reading this book. You'll be greater than a tourist!

-Alan Warner, Grand Rapids, USA

Thank you for a fantastic book.

-Don, Philadelphia, USA

Great ideas for a port day.

-Mary Martin USA

Even though I only have three days to spend in San Miguel in an upcoming visit, I will use the author's suggestions to guide some of my time there. An easy read - with chapters named to guide me in directions I want to go.

-Robert Catapano, USA

Great insights from a local perspective! Useful information and a very good value!

-Sarah, USA

This series provides an in-depth experience through the eyes of a local. Reading these series will help you to travel the city in with confidence and it'll make your journey a unique one.

-Andrew Teoh, Ipoh, Malaysia

GREATER THAN A TOURIST – MUNICH BAVARIA GERMANY

50 Travel Tips from a Local

Velimir Ilicic

Velimir Ilicic

Cover designed by Ivana Stamenković
Cover images: https://pixabay.com/en/bavaria-state-capital-munich-63268/

Greater Than a Tourist
Visit our website at www.GreaterThanaTourist.com

Lock Haven, PA

ISBN: 9781980645443

>TOURIST

50 TRAVEL TIPS FROM A LOCAL

Velimir Ilicic

BOOK DESCRIPTION

Are you excited about planning your next trip?

Do you want to try something new?

Would you like some guidance from a local?

If you answered yes to any of these questions, then this Greater Than a Tourist book is for you.

Greater Than a Tourist- Munich Bavaria Germany by Velimir Ilicic offers the inside scoop on Munich. Most travel books tell you how to travel like a tourist. Although there is nothing wrong with that, as part of the Greater Than a Tourist series, this book will give you travel tips from someone who has lived at your next travel destination.

In these pages, you will discover advice that will help you throughout your stay. This book will not tell you exact addresses or store hours but instead will give you excitement and knowledge from a local that you may not find in other smaller print travel books.

Travel like a local. Slow down, stay in one place, and get to know the people and the culture. By the time you finish this book, you will be eager and prepared to travel to your next destination.

Velimir Ilicic

TABLE OF CONTENTS

Velimir Ilicic

9. VISIT A METZGEREI AT EXACTLY 12 PM
10. DRINK A MUG AT A BIERGARTEN
11. GO FOR A BICYCLE RIDE
12. ENJOY A HELL OF A VIEW
13. FELL THE ATMOSPHERE OF A SMALL CAFE IN MUNICH
14. GO UNDERWATER
15. ADMIRE THE ARCHITECTURE
16. MAKE TIME TO VISIT THE NEUSCHWANSTEIN CASTLE
17. USE MUNICH'S PUBLIC TRANSPORTATION TO GET AROUND
18. GO GROCERY SHOPPING AT VIKTUALIENMARKT
19. GET READY TO BE SURPRISED BY MUNICH'S POLICE
20. VISIT THE HELLABRUNN ZOO
21. BRING YOUR KIDS WITH YOU TO THE BESUCHERPARK
22. TRY OUT THE MUNICH HOP-ON HOP-OFF TOUR
23. VISIT ONE OF THE MANY SMALL ARTIFICIAL LAKES IN MUNICH
24. TAKE A TOUR OF THE WORLDS LARGEST SCIENCE ISLAND

Velimir Ilicic

DEDICATION

This book is dedicated to my uncle Sasa Radulovic. Thank you for making it possible for me to live and work in Munich, and for all of the support you didn't have to give, but still gave it!

Velimir Ilicic

ABOUT THE AUTHOR

Velimir Ilicic is a freelance writer who likes to spend time reading, training and writing. He loves to travel and learn about other cultures and ways of living. Velimir has spent two and a half years in Munich working for a moving company. Working in a different location every day has given him a chance to get to know the city and the people's mentality better than most locals. He finds the city of Munich to be a vibrant, rich and diverse place filled with friendly people. Velimir currently lives in Vienna, but he will never forget the years spent in Munich, which gave him a perspective that changed his life.

Velimir Ilicic

HOW TO USE THIS BOOK

The Greater Than a Tourist book series was written by someone who has lived in an area for over three months. The goal of this book is to help travelers either dream or experience different locations by providing opinions from a local. The author has made suggestions based on their own experiences. Please do your own research before traveling to the area in case the suggested places are unavailable.

Velimir Ilicic

FROM THE PUBLISHER

Traveling can be one of the most important parts of a person's life. The anticipation and memories that you have are some of the best. As a publisher of the Greater Than a Tourist book series, as well as the popular 50 Things to Know book series, we strive to help you learn about new places, spark your imagination, and inspire you. Wherever you are and whatever you do I wish you safe, fun, and inspiring travel.

Lisa Rusczyk Ed. D.
CZYK Publishing

Velimir Ilicic

OUR STORY

Traveling is a passion of the "Greater than a Tourist" series creator. Lisa studied abroad in college, and for their honeymoon Lisa and her husband toured Europe. During her travels to Malta, an older man tried to give her some advice based on his own experience living on the island since he was a young boy. She was not sure if she should talk to the stranger but was interested in his advice. When traveling to some places she was wary to talk to locals because she was afraid that they weren't being genuine. Through her travels, Lisa learned how much locals had to share with tourists. Lisa created the "Greater Than a Tourist" book series to help connect people with locals. A topic that locals are very passionate about sharing.

Velimir Ilicic

WELCOME TO
> TOURIST

Velimir Ilicic

INTRODUCTION

"Travel is fatal to prejudice, bigotry, and narrow mindedness., and many of our people need it sorely on these accounts."

~ Mark Twain

The most important thing to know before visiting Munich is that it is a modern and secure city, connected with many means of transportation and filled with historical sights. So I wouldn't worry too much about getting around the city. The best introduction is actually a piece of advice. The Bavarian people are a friendly but also a proud bunch. They will welcome you as a member of the family, but you should nevertheless learn a couple of German words. Since everything is written in German, of course, it will be beneficial in many ways for you to get to know the language. Everybody likes to hear a foreigner speak the domestic language, so this will earn you some extra points with the locals. If that is too much of a problem for you,

Velimir Ilicic

don't worry, as Munich is populated by educated and diverse people of many different backgrounds. So don't hesitate to speak English. Learn something new and have fun!

1. VISIT THE MOST BEAUTIFUL CITY SQUARE IN GERMANY

To get a sense of what makes Germany a great but also a hospitable country, you just need to visit Munich's central square, Marienplatz. Since the foundation of Munich in 1158, the Marienplatz is the center and heart of the city. In the beginning, it was intended to be a market where people sold everyday food, so the locals just called it "market". Marienplatz was also used for executions in the 15th century as it was the main square from the beginning. Munich is an old city, and this square was from the beginning the most important part of it, which of course means that there are plenty of magnificent buildings left to tell us stories about it. The impressive architecture of the New and the Old City Hall is sure to make you stand in awe of the capability of the German people to build wonders. But it is the German hospitality which is the most impressive. Out of the 1.34 million citizens living in Munich, 186 thousand are foreigners. You just need to take a walk down Marienplatz to acknowledge this fact, which will make you feel right at home.

2. LEARN A COUPLE OF GERMAN WORDS

Munich is the capital of a landlocked federal state of Germany, Bavaria. Bavarians are people proud of their history and language. This can be spotted in every part of the city. The number of Bavarian flags scattered around Munich clearly tells anybody visiting that they are strong and proud people. Saying a couple of words in German will definitely make the person you are talking to give you a big smile. By visiting Munich, you will have a unique opportunity to hear the Bavarian dialect of the German language. Here are some words to help you out:

Grüß Gott - greetings or good day

Schmarrn - nonsense, rubbish

I mog di - I like you

Pfiat di - bye-bye

Freilich - of course

Fleischpflanzerl - meatball

Brezl - pretzel

And the most important one in Bavaria: Prost - cheers!

3. HAVE BREAKFAST AT A BÄCKEREI

German bakeries are famous around Europe for their salties and sweets. You can find them at every corner in Munich, and the best thing is, they are always full of people. The most famous foods you can buy at a Bäckerei are Brötchen (bread rolls), Brezel (soft pretzel), Vollkornbrot (whole grain bread), Milchbrötchen (milk roll), Mohnkuchen (poppy seed cake), Bienenstich (bee sting), Berliner (donut), Puddingbrezel (pudding pretzel) and Streuselkuchen (streusel cake). Each of these is special in its own way, and if you get the opportunity, you should definitely try every one.

4. ENJOY NATURE NEAR THE CITY CENTER

Often called the Central Park of Europe, the Englischer Garten spreads over an area of 3.7 km2 (1.4 sq mi) (370 ha or 910 acres), and is home to many sights and attractions. It is often called the lung of Munich, because of the greenness that it provides. You don't have to go outside of the city to enjoy time in nature, just hop on a U-Bahn and enjoy the many features provided by this park. Located on a small island in the south of the garden is the famous Japanese Teahouse. It was built to celebrate the Olympic games which were held in Munich in 1972. One of the most popular attractions is an artificial stream, which produces a standing wave on which you can go surfing. There is also the Chinese Tower, which stands 25-metres tall, has 5 floors, and provides you with a sense of peace. So if you like to spend your time peacefully in nature, the Englischer Garten is the place to go to.

5. GO SHOPPING MUNICH STYLE

Every big western city offers a variety of places where you can go shopping, so does Munich. Whether its Olympia-Einkaufszentrum, Mira Einkaufszentrum, Oberpollinger or any of the shops in the city center, Munich has got you covered. These places are also the ones which are the most visited by the locals, so you can easily meet someone there and maybe get an advice or two about where to go next. All you need to make sure of is that your budget fits well with the prices, otherwise you are looking at a day of shop window gazing.

6. CHECK OUT THE LATEST IN AUTOMOTIVE TECHNOLOGY

If you come across a building that looks like it came out of a sci-fi movie, you are at the BMW Welt exhibition center. It offers you a glimpse at the newest models of their cars. The entrance is free, and you can even sit in the cars and admire the craftsmanship and design. The prices of these cars range from thirty to over one hundred thousand dollars, so not everybody has a chance like this. if you are lucky, you could catch a drift show often organized in front of this building by the BMW professional drivers. Across the street from BMW welt is a different exhibition. Known as the salad bowl or white cauldron, the silver futuristic building, right next to the exhibition center is the BMW museum, where you can see all the classics that came from BMW. Around 250.000 people visit the museum every year, so you should definitely check it out.

7. SEE A FOOTBALL MATCH

Everybody knows that the Germans are big football fans and Munich is home to the Bayern Munich football club and the less successful TSV 1860 Munich football club. Ask any Munich resident, and he will gladly explain to you why these two football clubs are so different and why the fans don't like each other. The hardcore fans of TSV 1860 often say that it is easy to cheer for a club with a budget as big as the one that Bayern Munich has. On the other hand, Bayern Munich fans are so many, that it is a common thing to see a Bayern Munich flag in front of peoples houses. But they both share the same stadium, the Allianz Arena. It is famous for being the first stadium in the world that can fully change the color of its exterior. This is possible because it is surrounded by inflated plastic panels which are illuminated during the match. It is a place where the fans bite their nails out of worry and cheer from the top of their lungs out of love for their club.

8. DON'T GO HOME WITHOUT A PAIR OF LEDERHOSEN

For special events, the Bavarians like to wear their traditional clothing, Dirndl Dresses, and Lederhosen. It is not uncommon to see a man wearing these as everyday clothing, but it is most common to see everybody wear them during Oktoberfest. If you catch yourself in Munich during Oktoberfest, you are definitely going to encounter seas of people dressed this way, all going in one direction, and looking forward to drinking some good quality beer. If you get a chance, you should definitely join them dressed the same way, because it will be an unforgettable experience.

9. VISIT A METZGEREI AT EXACTLY 12 PM

This is the time when almost all workers make a half hour break, and rush to the nearest Metzgerei. It literally means butchers shop, and it offers a variety of German specialties. The two most famous are Fleischpflanzerl and Leberkasse. You can have it served on a plate, but the common way to eat it is in a Semmel with ketchup or mustard. Get in line with the locals and get a sense of this ritual which is an everyday part of life in Munich. You cant say that you have been to Germany until you have tried this because it is authentic food and the atmosphere that a Metzgerei provides is 100 percent Bavarian.

10. DRINK A MUG AT A BIERGARTEN

Again, back to the beer, as it is a huge part of the Bavarian culture. Biergarten originated in Munich in the 19th century. Beer gardens are outdoor areas which are filled with tables and benches. People serve beer and traditional Bavarian food there, but beside good food and quality beer, it offers a great vibe and an amazing atmosphere. The locals spend their winters dreaming about summer and Biergartens. The most famous one is Hirschgarten, which has seatings for over 8000 people. If you get a chance, visit one at night, so that you can experience an illuminated Biergarten which is truly a sight to see. This is the perfect place to meet the locals and make new friends.

11. GO FOR A BICYCLE RIDE

Now, unless you came to Munich with a Bicycle, it would seem that this one would be tough, but again this wonderful city has got you covered. Munich has a bicycle hire system which is called Call a Bike. These bikes are mostly available around the ring-road called the Mittlerer Ring. If you by any chance came to visit with a bike, you will have to stay a couple of days if you want to take the full advantage of Munich's bicycle network. It is more than 1.200 km long. This accounts for more than 50% of the total length of Munich's road network. Many streets are exclusively bicycle streets with motor vehicles can drive only 30 km per hour. Try it out and get a sense of why Munich is called the bicycle capital of Germany.

12. ENJOY A HELL OF A VIEW

Built in the center of the Olympic Park, is the 291 m high, and 52.500 tons heavy Olympiaturm(Olympic Tower), so if you have a fear of heights, this may not be a sight for you. At 190 m, there is an observation platform where you can enjoy a beautiful view. The tower was opened in 1968, and it has registered over 35 million visitors. At 182 m there is a restaurant, which can host 230 people at once. The best thing about it is, that it spins. Don't worry, it won't ruin your lunch because a full revolution takes 53 min. The tower has two crazy fast elevators with a speed of 7 m/s, which have a capacity of about 30 people per car. It will take you about 30 seconds to get to the top. The tower is open every day from 09 am to 12 am.

13. FELL THE ATMOSPHERE OF A SMALL CAFE IN MUNICH

When you take a walk around Munich's hidden streets, you will come across a variety of small cafes which give out a vibe of a time gone by. The best thing about these cafes is that they are full of young and beautiful people of diverse backgrounds. You can experience the full effect of the vibrant atmosphere in the summer when there are streets filled with people enjoying themselves and loving life. Some of the most popular are Cafe Jasmin, Cafe Lotti, Cafe Luitpold, Stereo Cafe and Cole Porter Bar. Each of these will provide you with a great service and put a smile on your face for the rest of the day.

14. GO UNDERWATER

Located at the Olympia Park, is the mesmerizing underwater world of Sea Life, where you can experience more than 4000 animals from lakes, oceans, and rivers. Get a unique chance to see the daily feedings, all kinds of crabs, sharks and turtles. There is also a ten-meter long tunnel under the ocean water pool, which is truly a magnificent sight to see. Here you can educate yourself a little bit about the amazing world of these incredible creatures. If you have trouble with finding a place to take your children to, then this is the answer. There is also the possibility of throwing a birthday party for your kids. Be sure to take a camera with you, as you will surely make some beautiful shots.

15. ADMIRE THE ARCHITECTURE

Munich is a city with a rich history, and every city with a rich history has a special story to tell. The city stories are best told by the architecture. And what architecture it is. The impression you get when seeing these buildings is that somebody made a fairy tale come true. The facades are all painted in different colors. You don't need much to lift your mood when you are feeling down, just walk outside and give yourself a minute to soak up the vibrant colors. Aside from the buildings where people live, there are many architectural treasures all over the city. Here some of them: New Town Hall steeple with Marian column, The Frauenkirche, Theatinerkirche at Odeonsplatz, Asam Church, Palais Holstein and Palais Porcia. Each of these will teach you something new about German history.

16. MAKE TIME TO VISIT THE NEUSCHWANSTEIN CASTLE

Now, this castle is located 2 hours away from Munich, but it would be a crime not to put it on the list, as it is one one the most beautiful buildings in the world and is a part of Bavarian history. It is a 19th-century palace on a hill above the village of Hohenschwangau in southwest Bavaria. The building of the castle was ordered by Ludwig II of Bavaria as a retreat. Ludwig paid for the palace out of his pocket. This castle was built to be a home for the king until he died in 1886. It was open to the public after his death. Since then 61 million people have visited Neuschwanstein Castle. If you ever wondered what a castle from a fairy tale looks like, visiting

Neuschwanstein will give you the answer. The only problem is that you will not want to leave after seeing it for the first time.

17. USE MUNICH'S PUBLIC TRANSPORTATION TO GET AROUND

Think twice before jumping into a car, as there is a far better way to get around. Munich has a fantastically connected system of public transportation, which consists of a subway system called the U-Bahn, suburban trains called the S-Bahn, trams, and buses. If you are just visiting and sight-seeing, it would be best if you bought the daily ticket. It costs around 6,70€ and is good for all public transportation. It is possible to get from one end of the city to another in less than 40 minutes. The system is very easy to understand so you won't have a trouble finding any of the sights you are looking for. The best part is that you can travel through the city like a local, as the majority of Munich's citizens use the public transportation.

18. GO GROCERY SHOPPING AT VIKTUALIENMARKT

The autochthonous Bavarian market which offers along with the smiles of the hospitable bavarian people various products is a secluded oasis of healthy food, beautiful flowers, and tasty wine. It seems that it was built to complement its surroundings which give out a vibe of medieval times. in the summer it is ornamented with the green color of the trees and during winter by beautiful Christmas lights. Bring a bag with you and fill it with exotic spices, herbs, teas, honey, fish, and meat. Enjoy the vibrant atmosphere provided by the excited tourists and the friendly locals. This one of a kind market is open from 10 am to 6 pm on working days, and from 10 pm to 3 pm on Saturdays, so don't forget to check it out.

19. GET READY TO BE SURPRISED BY MUNICH'S POLICE

It is a well-known fact that people around the world have a certain fear of police, but Munich's police department is on a mission to make that fact a myth. If you get pulled over by the people who drive green and gray cars and wear green uniforms, what awaits is a sincere smile, a willingness to help you out and explain to you whatever it is that needs to be explained. If you have any questions at all, don't hesitate for a moment to ask them, as 90 percent of them speak English. They will treat you with respect and make you fell how every police officer should make you feel, safe.

Velimir Ilicic

20. VISIT THE HELLABRUNN ZOO

This Zoo is a zoological garden, and it spreads on 40 hectares of land. The water level here is high and the water is of very good quality, so the Zoo uses this water for its needs. It is located on the right side of the Isar river.Many of the enclosures are without cages so they use moat features to keep the animals in line. Some of the exotic animals you can see here are elk, giraffes, elephants, gorillas, bison and Arctic foxes. The Zoo offers many places to sit and enjoy a meal while looking at the captivated wilderness. If you came with a pet dog to Munich, no worries, as it is allowed to bring a dog inside with you. This Zoo was proclaimed the 4th best Zoo in Europe, and you should come an see why.

21. BRING YOUR KIDS WITH YOU TO THE BESUCHERPARK

The Besucherpark is located near the Munich airport. Its motives are complementary to the aviation industry. From small airplanes intended for children to the big relics of the past, the Besucherpark is a perfect place to for a family to visit. There is also a restaurant where you can peacefully sit, eat and drink while keeping an eye on your kids. A big watch tower overlooks all of the runways, so if you feel like climbing up the tower, you are going to get a sense of how this humongous airport breathes. Every couple of minutes an airplane filled with people flyes away in an unknown direction. Seeing this will mesmerize and glue you to the spot you are standing at.

22. TRY OUT THE MUNICH HOP-ON HOP-OFF TOUR

You may be wondering how can you manage to see all of the sights and attractions in a short period of time? Here is the answer, hop on a double-decker bus which takes you on a tour of Munich's most important and most visited sights. The downside is that you don't have any control over how much time you spend at a certain sight, but if you are in a hurry and don't want to miss anything in Munich, this is a solution for you. You can book a 1 or a 2-day tour which costs around 15 €. Meet new people who are, just like you, there to enjoy all of the things that Munich has to offer. Book a trip and you won't miss a thing in Munich.

23. VISIT ONE OF THE MANY SMALL ARTIFICIAL LAKES IN MUNICH

If you are visiting in the summer, you should definitely go for a dip at one of the many artificial lakes in Munich. They are all beautifully made, peaceful with plenty of trees, green land, and above all filled with friendly people. These places make you feel like they were built with the intention to bring people together. Join the people who are barbequing, they will surely be more than happy to welcome you and get to know you. One of the most beautiful ones in Munich is the Feldmochinger lake. It has a skate park, a beach volleyball field, a football field and many tables for ping pong. Go with your friends and have fun!

24. TAKE A TOUR OF THE WORLDS LARGEST SCIENCE ISLAND

What I mean by science island is actually, the Deutsches Museum. This, straight out of a movie looking building is home to more than 28 thousand exhibits from 50 fields of science and technology. It was founded on 28 June 1903 as an idea of Oskar von Miller, who was a German electrical engineer, mostly known for building a high voltage line from Miesbach to Munich in 1882. The Deutsches Museum is located on a small island in the Isar river and was for some time to host rock and pop concerts. The tours are available in English and German, so you shouldn't miss out on the fascinating exhibits and history of this incredible museum.

25. VISIT THE DACHAU CONCENTRATION CAMP

The Dachau concentration camp is located some 20 minutes from Munich. It was one of the first concentration camps that were open at the beginning of WWII. Its purpose was to keep political prisoners and forced labor inside. Like many of the camps during that time, it was a place where many people of various nationalities and backgrounds have lost their lives by way of torture, hanging and being shot. It is estimated that 32000 people have lost their lives here, and thousands more that are not documented. The people who were locked up there lived in fear of torment. This camp should be visited to remind us of the atrocities that were being committed by the fascists in that time and to pay respect to the victims of this monstrous political regime.

26. ENJOY A NIGHT OF CULTURE

Munich is home to the Gasteig cultural center, where numerous concerts and plays are being held. It has 4 halls which can host altogether around 3400 people. Here you can see a number of international plays and concerts. It is also the home of the Munich Philharmonic Orchestra and is a host of the Munich Filmfest. The Philharmonic Hall is built in a shape of seashell and mostly out of wood, which makes this a romantic place where you could bring your partner with. If you enjoy a night at the theater, the Gasteig cultural center will not disappoint you.

27. VISIT THE CASTLE OF THE NYMPH

In 1826, the building of the Schloss Nymphenburg was completed. This baroque palace was a residence of the rulers of Bavaria. It somewhat resembles the Schönbrunn Palace located in Vienna but what makes it unique is its beautiful park and the long water canal which leads to the marble cascade. This palace is an oasis of peace and silence. If you find yourself in Munich and you need a time-out, this is the right choice. A common thing to see here is people running, which makes sense considering the fact that this park covers 229 square kilometers of land. inside tours of the castle are also available year round. The Buildings interior takes you back in history and helps you understand what kind of luxury these people enjoyed.

28. TAKE A DRIVE DOWN LUDWIGSTRASSE

If you like to treat yourself to a little luxury, the Ludwigstrasse is the destination you should visit. This street is filled with world-renowned fashion stores. Some of the most beautiful buildings are homes to these stores, and this contributes to the overall feeling of exclusiveness and class. Not only that, some of the worlds most expensive cars have their shops opened there as well. If your wallet is thinning out, then shopping here is not for you. On the other hand, there are many other features this street has to offer. The most distinctive one is at the beginning of the street, which is, of course, the Siegestor. This magnificent Triumphal gate with three arches and the statue of Bavaria on top will make you feel like royalty as you drive by it. Located here is also the monumental Ludwigskirche.

29. VISIT THE FAMOUS OKTOBERFEST

The Oktoberfest is known worldwide for the amount of beer that people drink in the two weeks of its duration. This festival has its roots deep in the Bavarian culture and is an important part of Munich's tourism. It has been held since 1810. There many things to do on Oktoberfest alongside drinking beer. It is filled with amusement rides and games, something similar to Vienna's Prater. It is estimated that some 7.7 millions of liters of beer are being served and 6.7 million people come to visit every year. The best thing about Oktoberfest is a positive atmosphere. Every time you go there, you cant feel down, as the cheerfulness of the crowd will make you want to be friends with everybody there. The beautiful blonde haired waitresses, dressed in traditional Bavarian clothing will bring you bear, the traditional Bavarian music will be played, and you will wish you could stay forever.

30. TAKE A WALK ALONG THE ISAR RIVER

If you like long walks in calming ambiances, I've got the perfect thing for you. The Isar river runs through Munich and split it beautifully in half. This river alone can cost you a day spent there because of its features. The already mentioned Deutsches museum has its place on an island located in the middle of the river. Not only that, you can actually go surfing on this river. There is a standing wave right by the

Wittelsbacherbrücke. If you are visiting in the summer, visit the beach by the river, where many people go for a barbeque, relax after a working day and they even take a dip in this wide and beautiful river. But it is the calmness of the boardwalk by the river which gives the best possibility to go for a romantic walk with a loved one or just relax by yourself and slow down the happenings around you.

31. JOIN SOME PEOPLE IN A GAME OF FOOTBALL

Germany is well known for its success in football. You can clearly see why when you notice how much they invest in the development of this sport. Every part of the city has one or two smaller clubs, and many football fields that are open for local people to use. Whether it is a grass field or one coved with concrete, they are all filled with people giving their best on the pitch. If you can make time for an activity like this you should try it out, break a sweat, and maybe even learn a couple of German words. The best way to connect with the Germans is through football, and if you are any good at it, you will be praised and surely invited to come and play again.

Velimir Ilicic

32. TRY OUT THE GERMAN AUTOBAHN

Autobahn is a German word for highway, but there are some differences between a normal highway and a German one. The first thing is, they are built like airplane runways. A known fact in Europe is that used cars which have been driven in Germany are the best ones and the quality of their streets and highways is the reason why. Another thing that separates Germany from others when it comes to driving on a highway is that there are often no speed limits. This is the reason why you can often see somebody fly by you going over 200 km per hour. If you own a fast car, and you like to give it a true test, take it out for a quick drive down the German Autobahn, and be amazed by how precise Geman engineering is.

33. GO TO OLYMPIAPARK WITH YOUR FRIENDS

The beautiful Olympiapark is one the most visited sights in Munich. It was built in the summer of 197 when the Olympic games were being held there. It is located right next to the futuristic BMW Welt and consists of four portions. The first one is the monumental Olympic stadium which can host 80.000 people and where European and World cups were held. Many events such as concerts and shows are still held at this stadium, so if you are passing by when something is going on there, be sure to check it out. The second portion is the already mentioned shopping center. The third portion is the Olympic Village which was used to host athletes during the Olympics and is now home to many of Munich's citizens. The last portion is the Olympic park. It is a place where many families and friends go during the weekend in search of a good time. Go and see why this is the most family-friendly environment in Munich.

Velimir Ilicic

34. GO HIKING IN THE GERMAN ALPS

If you are Staying in Munich for longer than a weekend you should drive to Garmisch-Partenkirchen and spend a day hiking. If you have a car with you it will take about an hour to get there, if not hop on a direct train. Garmisch-Partenkirchen is a beautiful and small town filled with friendly people who are there for you if you have any questions. The 6-hour walk to the summit of Wank is going to give your legs a good workout for the day. The peak itself is at an altitude of 1050 m. A jaw-dropping view and refreshments await you there, so don't miss out.

35. BE OPEN TO NEW PEOPLE

The Germans, especially in Munich like it when people are direct and don't beat around the bush. If you are in a need of help ask a local on the street or ring a doorbell, and the solution will provide itself through the politeness and the willingness of the locals to help you out. You haven't been greeted properly if you haven't been to Munich. Just try to make contact with some people your age, and a new Munich will shine its light on you. Nobody can help you experience the city like the people who live there, so try to meet as many of them as possible. The thing that makes a city what it is, are its citizens.

36. DISCOVER THE WORLD OF GERMAN ENGINEERING

If you are a tech geek then Germany is the country for you. It is the home of 6 biggest car companies in the world, and Munich is home to BMW. Every couple of years each of the car companies reveal their latest models which are going to be sold all over the world. When you take a seat in any of them, a different approach to making cars is revealed to you. The details and the craftsmanship are miles away from the competition. These masterpieces of engineering have a German soul embedded in them. If you find yourself crossing the Hackerbrucke bridge, you will often see a train loaded with BMWs all ready to be sold all over the world. The best thing about wanting to sit in a BMW in Munich is that it is possible. Just visit the BMW Welt or any of their shops in Munich, and some lovely people will explain everything you want to know about the car you are sitting in.

37. GO OUT AND ENJOY MUNICH'S NIGHTLIFE

When you are young, the most interesting thing to you is probably going to be the nightlife of a city. Well, Munich has a large variety of places for you to go and enjoy yourself. From underground clubs to the exclusive ones you can really pick and choose what is your cup of tea. The first one you should consider is the 80ies reloaded bar. It has a funky design, offers a large choice of drinks and fair prices. If you are an alternative type, you should visit the Backstage club. This club is everything but exclusive. Here you can hear all types of alternative music from reggae to heavy metal. There is also the "Cohiba". You should be prepared for a night of dancing. A vibrant club packed with energetic people is going to live its mark on you, and you will surely want to come back again.

38. GO BACK IN TIME AT THE FILMTHEATER SENDLINGER TOR

Along with the modern movies which can be watched at every cinema, there is a classical side to the Sendlinger movie theater. On Sundays, this lovely place gives you a chance to experience all the emotions provided by the opera and ballet. It is a contemporary witness of film history which was first opened in 1913. This theatre has undergone many changes throughout the years and is a monument of culture in Munich. It is the only place in Munich that has kept the classics alive and intends to do so in the future. A perfect place to spend an unforgettable night with your partner, which is surely not going to be forgotten.

39. DRIVE OUT TO THE BAVARIA SEA

Approximately 80 km from Munich is the Chiemsee lake, also known as the Bavarian Sea. The Chiemsee lake got the nickname because of its size. It covers an area of 80 square kilometers and includes 4 islands. This spectacle formed by nature is a perfect place to spend a day with your family, or just enjoy a day of peace and quiet. Many people drive out every weekend during the summer from places located far from the lake, which really proves that this is a beautiful destination. among many activities which are available at the lake, you will have a chance to give paragliding a try, if you are a bit on the extreme side of course. The most important thing you should have in mind when visiting Chiemsee is to take you swimming suit with you, forget your daily worries and have fun.

40. LEARN A FEW THINGS ABOUT THE CITY

This one is to do when you are actually there. The best way to learn something is with a hands-on approach. If you are interested in history, and how we came to be as developed as we are, then Munich will have a few things to tell you. It was founded as a medieval town in 1158 and some buildings still stand today as proof of this. Throughout history, Munich has witnessed many happenings which shaped the world we live in today. The Nazi party was formed in Munich by Hitler, and if you get to talk about this with a local, you can evidently see how heavy of a burden that is for the German people. But when you take a walk around the city, you can see how much they have done to help themselves and everybody else forget their terrible past. It is amazing to see a nations commitment to move forward and prosper, and this is something that Germans do best.

41. VISIT THE JÜDISCHES MUSEUM

If you are a history geek, then this museum will definitely fulfill your need for knowledge. It is a museum of Jewish history which will give you an insight into Jewish life and religion. The original museum was humbly open to visitors in 1980 by a group of people who believed that Munich deserves a museum like this. The one we can see today was opened in 2007 and has a modern look to it. It has three exhibition floors here really educate yourself about the Jewish culture. Don't hesitate to ask questions as they will surely be answered. You will notice that the exhibits are not placed systematically, but they managed somehow to perfectly present the Jewish culture which is a prehistorical one. After a tour is done, you will truly feel enriched by the amount of knowledge collected at this place, not just about the Jewish culture, but also about culture in general, as it has its roots in the Jewish history.

42. WATCH OUT FOR THE BLITZER

Munich is known for having many traffic cameras posted all around the city. This is why many of its citizens often get headaches when receiving their mail. It a normal thing to receive a ticket for speeding once or twice a month. The most common place for the cameras to be is the 30 zone, as people often get carried away by the quality of the road and the car they are driving. Munich is a truly rich city, and you will acknowledge this fact as soon as you see which type of car an average citizen drives. To help you out with the location of the Blitzer are the citizens of Munich, through a simple telephone call to the radio. Every day people call the radio in solidarity, to inform you where they have been blitzed. Foreigners will also receive a ticket at their address no matter where they live, so you better watch out. The best advice for this is to follow the traffic rules without exception, otherwise, a visit to Munich might cost you more than you thought.

43. TAKE A WHIFF AT THE BOTANISCHER GARTEN

People often ask where they can go and see something unique when visiting a city. Well, one of the best places in Munich is the Nymphenburg Botanical garden. It was opened in 1809 and is located in the Menzinger Str. 65. This magnificent place cultivates around 13.000 plants. It covers 18 hectares and is mostly used for educational purposes. A collection of 2700 species of orchids can be seen there. With 11 greenhouses covering a space of 4.500 square meters, it is the biggest botanical garden in Germany. This is the place where one should take time to observe the colorfulness and the beauty that is being preserved by the botanists of the Botanischer Garten.

44. TRY NOT TO GET LOST

This, of course, applies to the Munich airport. If you are flying to Munich, you will most surely land on a Munich Airport runway. What awaits you there, is the worlds 15th-busiest airport. This humongous airport has two terminals and these two combined handle around 42 million passengers annually. It has two runways 4.000 meters long and a helipad. You can also grab a bite to eat or go shopping at the Munich Airport Center which connects the two terminals. Trying to navigate around this airport can be a tricky task. The good thing is that there are always friendly people, positioned at every corner of the airport waiting to answer any question you might have.

45. MAKE A BARGAIN AT THE OLYMPIAPARK FLOHMARKT

When driving by the Olympiastadium on a Saturday, people visiting Munich often ask their hosts why are there so many people in the huge parking lot. Well, they are trying to find what they need for the lowest price possible. That is the reason why Munich flea market is so popular. The locals often say that you can find anything from a needle to a locomotive there, and that is almost true. If you came to Munich to stay for a longer period, this is the place to begin searching for all the pieces that make an apartment a home. As mentioned before, Munich is truly a rich city, therefore the stuff being sold at the Flohmarkt is mostly of high quality. People who are on a budget but want a bicycle, go to the Flohmarkt because they know that it is the place where they can make a good deal. It is not unusual to find brand new clothes or furniture as well. It is usually open on Fridays and Saturdays from 9 am to 3 pm. So if you are a fan of used stuff this is definitely a place you should put on your visiting list.

Velimir Ilicic

46. HANG OUT AT THE FRIEDENSENGE

This piece of history dating back to 1895, which commemorates the end of the German-French War of 1870-71 is one of the more popular places for young people to hang out at. For couples in love or just a group of friends trying to get away from sight, this monument offers a secluded space for the ones who are aware of it. Leading to this monument is the Luitpold Bridge which contributes to the already mesmerizing charm of this area. In the center is a fountain resembling some of the more beautiful squares in Europe. The monument itself was built to resemble the ancient Greek monuments and temples. A perfect place for newcomers to get a feel for Munich heartbeat and charm. They say that when you want to get a girl to like you, you should bring her here at dusk and let the charm of the Friedensenge do the trick.

47. VISIT THE MERCEDES-BENZ SHOWROOM

One of the first things that people notice in Munich is a huge building with a glass exterior which has a majority of Mercedes-Benz cars exhibited as a part of it. It is the Mercedes center and offers you a chance to take a look at latest and the oldest cars produced by this gigantic company. It is a huge part of the automotive history, starting with the smaller cars and limousines to the trucks and busses. The Mercedes showroom located in this building pays an homage to the history of this company and shows a window to its future. Here you will get a unique chance to sit in vehicles worth over hundred thousand dollars and for a couple of minutes experience first hand what it feels like to own a car like this. If you are a petrol head then this is the place you should put on your visiting list because it will be a memorable one.

48. SPEND A DAY AT THE NORDBAD SWIMMING POOL

There are many public swimming pools in Munich, but none of them come close to the Nordbad in regards to quality and originality. It is located in the Schleißheimer Straße in a part of the city called Schwabing-West. This beautiful building was opened in 1941 and was built in a neoclassical style of architecture, resembling the buildings from ancient Greece. It offers a spa, one Olympic swimming pool and an outside pool with hot water where you can relax even during winter. It is especially interesting in the evenings as the pools are lited up with underwater lights. The biggest problem with public swimming pools is that there are always too many people, but with Nordbadd you won't have that problem. No matter what part of the day it is there is always a reasonable amount of people there. Be sure to treat yourself to a relaxing day at the magnificent Nordbad.

49. TURN YOUR LIFE UPSIDE DOWN

A short 30 thirty minute drive away from Munich is the breathtaking and thrilling Skyline Park. This amusement park is filled with rides designed to fulfill every adrenalin desire. It offers a variety of rollercoasters for every age. The main attraction of this park is, of course, the Sky Wheel. The train is pulled vertically upwards until it goes into the overhead position at the top. Then follows a 360 ° turn from overhead to overhead, then the vertical descent through the station. This thrilling ride alone is enough to make thrill seekers come all over the world just for this one ride. Along the SkyWheel are also Sky Spin, Kids Spin, Sky Dragster, Bob Racing, Sky Fall, Sky Shot, Sky Walk, Achterbahn, High Fly, Sky Circle, Sky Rider, Sky Jet all of which offer great fun and lots of adrenaline. This is a perfect place to visit if you came to Munich with kids as they will surely enjoy it.

50. LIVE IN THE MOMENT

Now this one should be implemented every day, but people need to be reminded of this especially if they plan on visiting Munich. Every part of this wonderful and inspiring city invites you to activate your senses in order to soak up all of its offerings and allow yourself to fall in love with it. Whether it be during the summer or winter, Munich has something for everyone. A rich cultural and art scene, beautiful parks and squares, a magnificent history and friendly and hospitable people. This visit will leave you full of impressions and give you a new understanding of the German mentality. Grab a friend or a partner, explore the city, don't stop until the sun sets, and when the night falls go out again and experience the nightlife of Munich. Munich will be the city you will always carry in your heart and a city which you will always want to visit again. Enjoy it!

TOP REASONS TO BOOK THIS TRIP

The People: The Bavarian people will stay in your heart forever

The Food: Delicious and unique food

Architecture: The old buildings of Munich came out of a fairytale.

Velimir Ilicic

> TOURIST
GREATER THAN
A TOURIST

Visit GreaterThanATourist.com:
http://GreaterThanATourist.com

Sign up for the Greater Than a Tourist Newsletter:
http://eepurl.com/cxspyf

Follow us on Facebook:
https://www.facebook.com/GreaterThanATourist

Follow us on Pinterest:
http://pinterest.com/GreaterThanATourist

Follow us on Instagram:
http://Instagram.com/GreaterThanATourist

Follow on Twitter:
http://twitter.com/ThanaTourist

Velimir Ilicic

> TOURIST
GREATER THAN
A TOURIST

Please leave your honest review of this book on Amazon and Goodreads. Thank you. We appreciate your positive and constructive feedback. Thank you.

Velimir Ilicic

NOTES

Printed in Great Britain
by Amazon